CHRISTMAS Fun!
BIBLE ACTIVITY BOOK

(Based on Luke 1—2, Matthew 1—2)

Written by: Wendy van Leeuwen

Illustrated by: Wes Molebash

Scripture quotations taken from the HOLY BIBLE, NEW INTERNATIONAL VERSION ®. NIV®. Copyright © 1973, 1978, 1984, 2011 by Biblica, Inc.®. Used by permission. All rights reserved worldwide.

The purchase of this coloring book grants you the rights to photocopy the contents for classroom use. Notice: It is unlawful to copy these pages for resale purposes. Copy permission is for private use only.

Copyright © 2015 Warner Press, Inc. All rights reserved. Made in USA

Warner Press Kids
educate · nurture · inspire
www.warnerpress.org

305800210249

A messenger told Mary she would have a very special baby. His name would be Jesus, and He would be God's own Son. Who was the messenger?

Color by number to finish the picture.

1=White
2=Orange
3=Yellow
4=Brown
5=Black

6=Blue
7=Red
8=Green
9=Purple
10=Pink

How surprised Mary must have been to hear the angel's amazing news! She had been chosen to be the mother of God's Son, Jesus. What did the angel say about Jesus?

Start at the bold **H** in the corner and write it on the first space below. Then follow the arrow to find out which letter comes next. Write down each letter until you've discovered the entire message.

H→	E↓	N→	D→	W→	I↓
O↓	W↓	A↑	T←	M←	L↓
L↓	I←	E→	A↑	B↓	L←
L↓	P↑	R↑	K↑	E↓	C↑
B→	E→	G↑	F↓	C→	A↓
N↓	O←	H↓	T←	B←	L↓
O↓	S↑	E←	D↑	E←	L←
F↓	E→	M↓	L↓	S↑	Q←
T→	H↑	O↓	W↓	I→	G↓
P←	J↓	S→	T→	H↑	H.

_ _ _ _ _ _ _ _ _ _ _ _

_ _ _ _ _ _ _ _ _ _ _ _ _ _

_ _ _ _ _ _ _ _ _ _ _ _ .

Luke 1:32

(Answers on page 16)

God chose a man named Joseph to be Jesus' earthly father. He was a godly man who was part of King David's family. Joseph made his living as a carpenter.

Fit the words below into the crossword grid.

Hint: count the number of letters to help you decide where they should go.

| carving | nails | sander | file | plane |
| saw | hammer | rasp | wood | level |

(Answers on page 16)

An angel appeared to Joseph in a dream and told him Mary would have a very special baby—God's own Son. He would be called Immanuel.

Starting at the outside end of the spiral, write every third letter (3, 6, 9...) on the lines below to find out what Immanuel means.

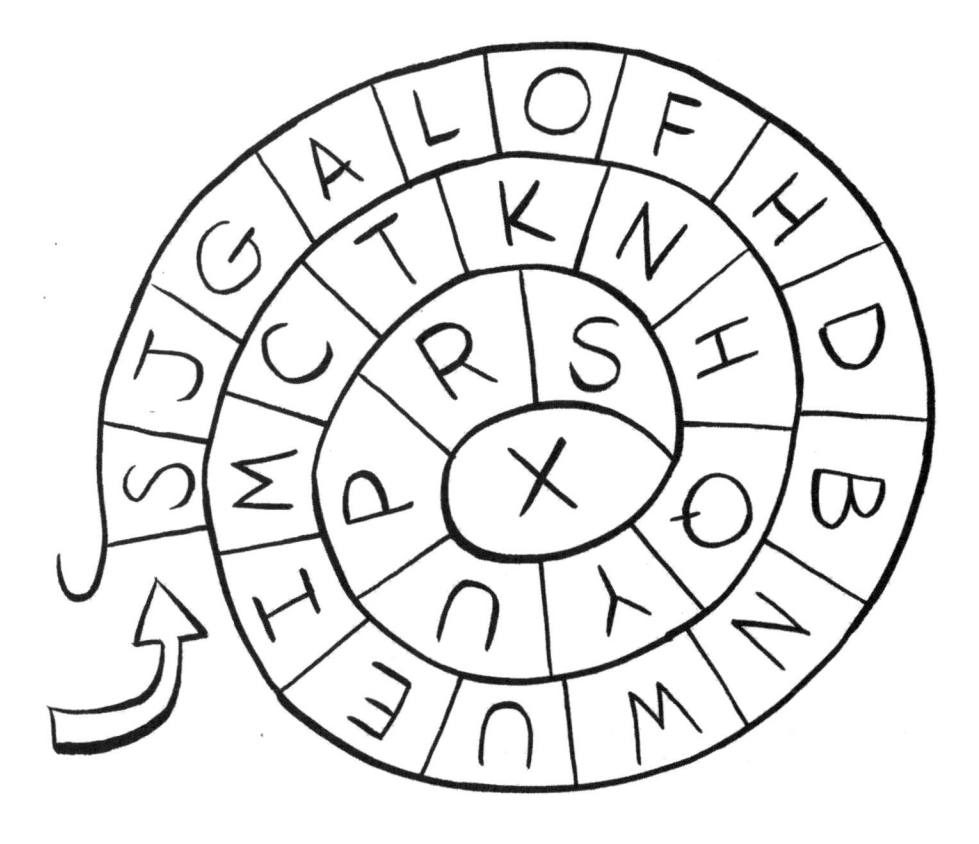

___ ___ ___ ___ ___ ___ ___ ___. Matthew 1:23

(Answers on page 16)

© 2015 Warner Press, Inc All rights reserved E4771

Joseph and Mary went to Bethlehem because the ruler of Rome wanted to know how many people lived in his empire. It was a long, difficult journey—especially for Mary, who would have a baby soon. Maybe she rode a donkey while Joseph walked in front.

Today we have many ways to travel from place to place. Can you unscramble these transportation words?

ATRNI _____

TBAO _____

ETFE _____

ARC _____

SUB _____

LNEPIRAA _____

EKBI _____

(Answers on page 16)

When Mary and Joseph got to Bethlehem, the only place they could find to rest was in the stable behind an inn. When Jesus was born, His parents wrapped Him in strips of cloth and laid Him in a manger.

Shade in the numbered squares according to the key.

(Answers on page 16)

© 2015 Warner Press, Inc All rights reserved E4771

A stable is an animal shed. It was a humble place for the Son of God to be born. Perhaps some animals watched Jesus as He slept in their feedbox.

Can you match these animal mothers with their babies?

MARE	CUB
COW	CHICK
BEAR	LAMB
SWAN	FOAL
KANGAROO	CYGNET
SHEEP	CALF
CAT	GOSLING
FISH	PUPPY
GOOSE	KITTEN
DOG	JOEY
HEN	FINGERLING

(Answers on page 16)

Some shepherds watching their sheep in the fields were the first to hear the good news. Angels told them, "Today in the town of David a Savior has been born to you; he is Christ the Lord" (Luke 2:11).

Which two sheep are exactly the same? Look carefully!

(Answers on page 16)

The frightened shepherds listened in amazement as angels filled the night sky with praise to God. Then they ran to Bethlehem to see Baby Jesus for themselves.

Fit the letter blocks into the spaces to spell out the angels' message. Some letters have been filled in for you.

(Answers on page 16)

When Jesus was eight days old, His parents named Him in a special ceremony.

Can you find and circle these other names of Jesus?

```
N S C F H H V Y P M J O M M K J T T W I U L T U K
U A L P E A S C D D B N A O J I Z C G H U Y P S G
L V B E Z B Q Y R O E G M B I B C H R I S T R C D
J I H D V E N T V S M O W M E S S I A H F R I O E
C O C C L O R D H B O O Y P R K A T K T K H N U J
D R S D S N E J V O Q D F X B O D X V S M K C N O
Q S W X S E V E R L A S T I N G F A T H E R E S M
G Q Q M W W S D C D P H U V W Q S M F I L L O E Q
P N U F V O B L O R F E M G L Z C I U U P R F L Y
I G N C B S N K V C G P T A Z Z Q G W T N I P O Z
G Y A U K C H D C O E H V A M R B H B C M B E R X
Y A O O P J L F E G E E G N U P J T U A C U A W S
N F B H F L Y V R I R J W F V O Y O J Z S C G X
Q Q V F K N Y I K N F D P M K N Q G A N I F E B W
X N Y E D X T S F H V U M E G S O O Z N I H D V I
A K S I Y D H C Q P I F L H M B K D Z J Y S O D I
M P R V A E F A J H Y P O R S C S A B I L T M R D
```

Wonderful   Counselor   Mighty God   Everlasting Father   Prince of Peace
Good Shepherd   Savior   Messiah   Christ   Lord

(Answers on page 16)

JESUS' parents brought Him to the TEMPLE to dedicate Him to GOD. An old man named SIMEON took Jesus is his arms and praised God. "Sovereign LORD, as you have PROMISED, you may now dismiss your SERVANT in PEACE. For my eyes have seen your SALVATION, which you have prepared in the sight of all NATIONS: a LIGHT for revelation to the GENTILES, and the GLORY to your people ISRAEL" (Luke 2:29-32).

Fit the words above in CAPITAL letters into the puzzle grid.
Hint: count the number of letters. All spaces needing a letter S have been filled in to get your started.

(Answers on page 16)

A wonderful new star appeared in the sky when Jesus was born. In a distant country, wise men (called Magi) saw the star and knew it meant a new king had been born in Judea.

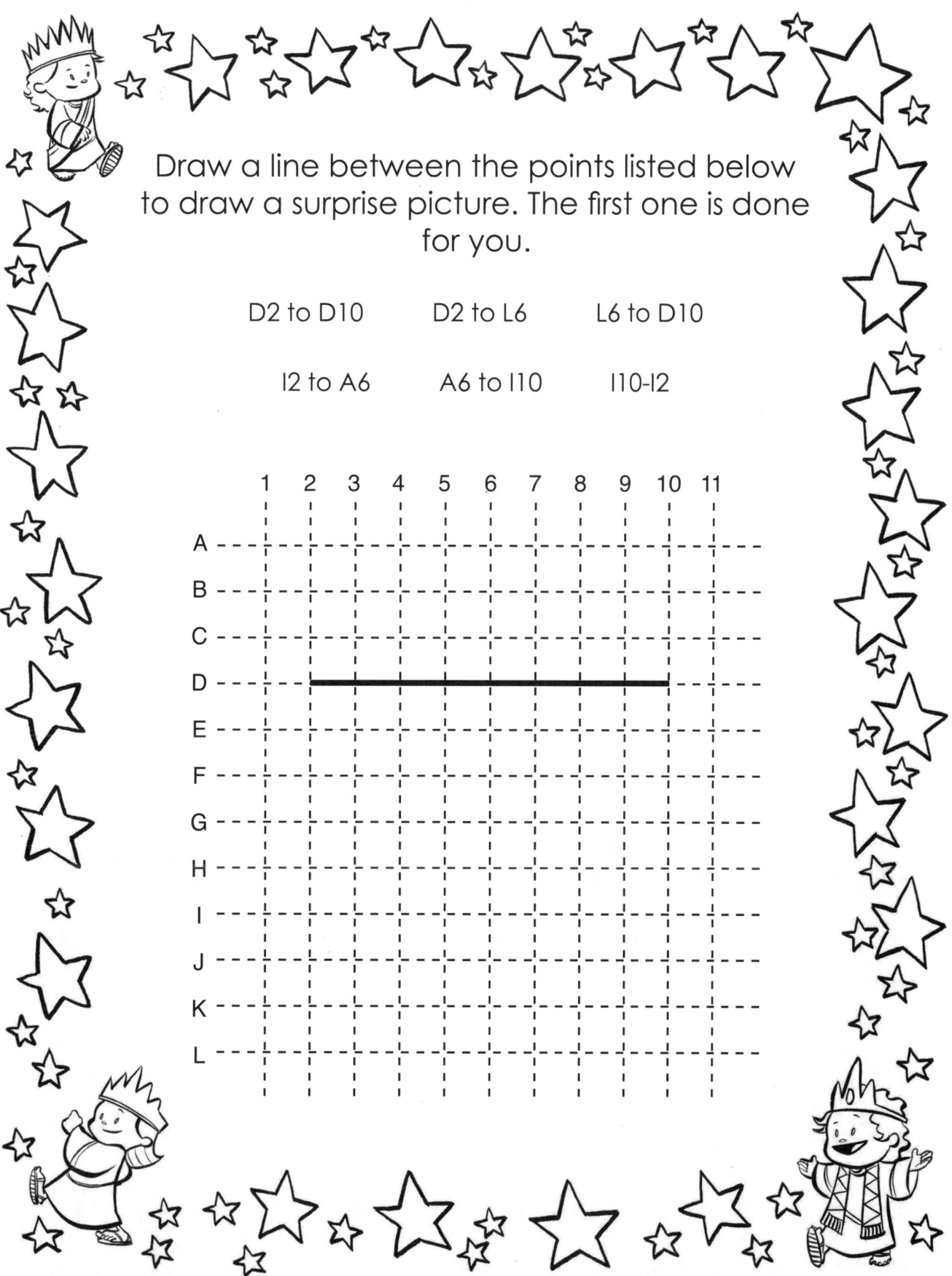

Draw a line between the points listed below to draw a surprise picture. The first one is done for you.

D2 to D10   D2 to L6   L6 to D10

I2 to A6   A6 to I10   I10-I2

(Answers on page 16)

© 2015 Warner Press, Inc All rights reserved   E4771

The Magi followed the star from their home in the East to Jerusalem. They visited King Herod and asked Him about the new King of the Jews.

All of the answers to these clues end with the word KING. Do you know them all?

1. Doing a job. ___ ___ ___ KING
2. Preparing a cake in an oven. ___ ___ KING
3. Pretending. ___ ___ KING
4. Seeing something. ___ ___ ___ KING
5. Telling a funny story. ___ ___ KING
6. Preparing food on the stove. ___ ___ ___ KING
7. Pedaling a two-wheeler. ___ ___ KING
8. Using words to communicate. ___ ___ ___ KING
9. Opening and closing your eyes quickly. ___ ___ ___ ___ KING
10. Traveling to another place on foot. ___ ___ ___ KING

(Answers on page 16)

The Magi traveled to Bethlehem to worship Jesus. They brought gold, frankincense, and myrrh—the first Christmas presents.

Connect the dots to finish the picture.

ANSWERS

Page 3

He will be great and will be called the Son of the Most High.   Luke 1:32

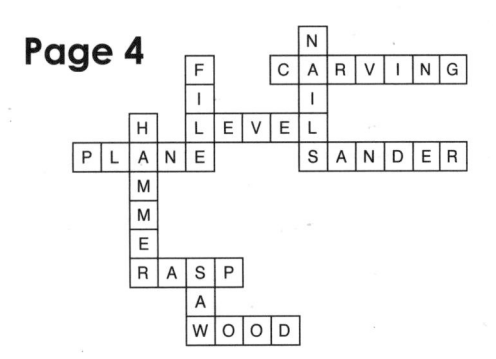

Page 4

Crossword answers: CARVING, FILE, LEVEL, NIL, HAMMER, PLANE, SANDER, RASP, SAW, WOOD

Page 5

God with us.

Page 6

TRAIN
BOAT
FEET
CAR
BUS
AIRPLANE
BIKE

Page 7

Page 8

MARE > FOAL
COW > CALF
BEAR > CUB
SWAN > CYGNET
KANGAROO > JOEY
SHEEP > LAMB
CAT > KITTEN
FISH > FINGERLING
GOOSE > GOSLING
DOG > PUPPY
HEN > CHICK

Page 9

Page 10

Glory to God in the highest, on earth peace to men on whom His favor rests.   Luke 2:14

Page 11

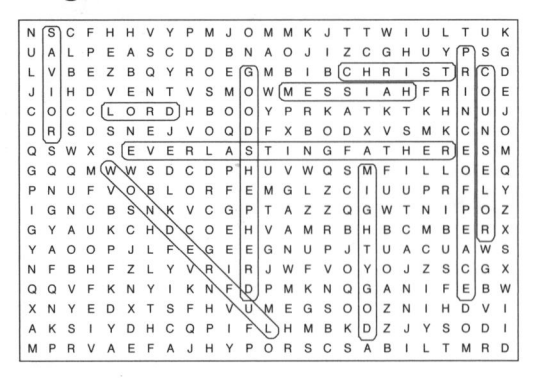

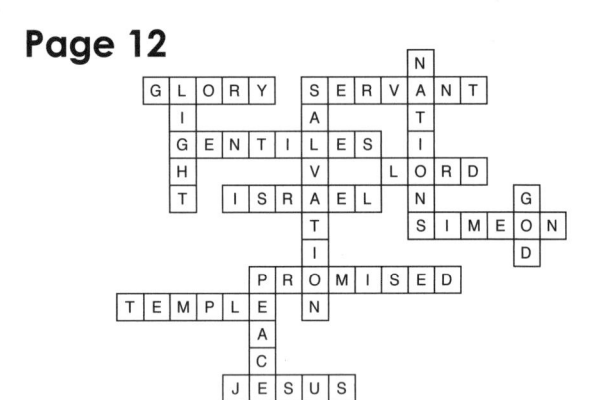

Page 12

Crossword answers: GLORY, SERVANT, LIGHT, SALVATION, GENTILES, LORD, ISRAEL, GOD, SIMEON, PROMISED, TEMPLE, PEACE, JESUS

Page 13

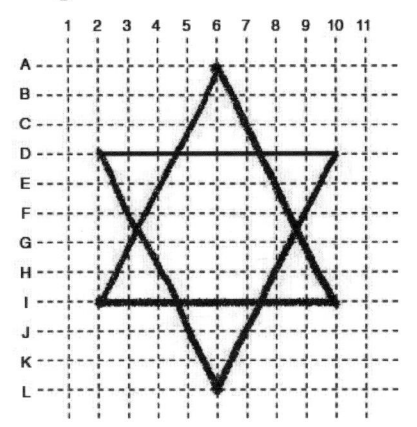

Page 14

WORKING
BAKING
FAKING
LOOKING
JOKING
COOKING
BIKING
TALKING
BLINKING
WALKING

© 2015 Warner Press, Inc All rights reserved   E4771